THE GREAT WHITE SHARK

BY LISA OWINGS

BELLWETHER MEDIA • MINNEAPOLIS, MN

Jump into the cockpit and take flight with Pilot Books. Your journey will take you on high-energy adventures as you learn about all that is wild, weird, fascinating, and fun!

This edition first published in 2012 by Bellwether Media, Inc.

No part of this publication may be reproduced in whole or in part without written permission of the publisher. For information regarding permission, write to Bellwether Media, Inc., Attention: Permissions Department, 5357 Penn Avenue South, Minneapolis, MN 55419.

Library of Congress Cataloging-in-Publication Data

Owings, Lisa.
 The great white shark / by Lisa Owings.
   p. cm. – (Pilot books. Nature's deadliest)
 Includes bibliographical references and index.
 Summary: "Fascinating images accompany information about the great white shark. The combination of high-interest subject matter and narrative text is intended for students in grades 3 through 7"–Provided by publisher.
 ISBN 978-1-60014-665-7 (hardcover : alk. paper)
 1. White shark–Juvenile literature. I. Title.
 QL638.95.L3O95 2012
 597.3'3–dc22   2011011674

Printed in the United States of America, North Mankato, MN.

080111   1187

CONTENTS

IN THE JAWS OF DEATH

On December 8, 1963, Rodney Fox was competing in a spearfishing tournament off Aldinga Beach in southern Australia. As he swam through the water, he spotted a fish and took a deep breath. He dove after it, letting out the line that tied him to his **float**. Fox aimed his speargun and prepared to fire.

Suddenly, something slammed into the left side of his body. The force knocked the speargun out of his hands and ripped the mask from his face. Fox was in the massive jaws of a great white shark. The animal's jagged teeth sunk into his **torso**. Water swirled around Fox's ears as the shark dragged him faster and faster through the water. His lungs began to fill with blood, and the water around him was turning red.

Killer Reputation

The great white shark is commonly called "the man-eater" or "white death."

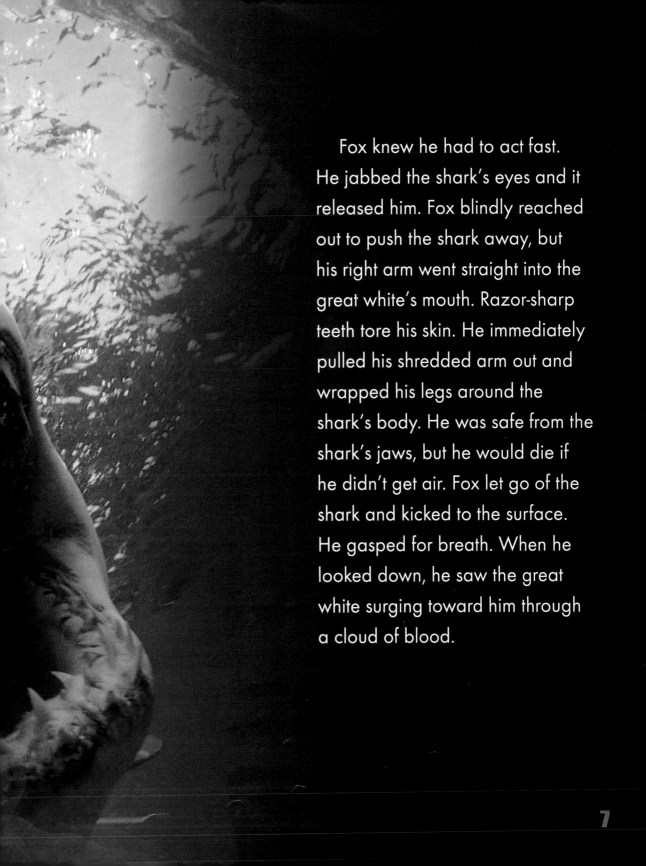

Fox knew he had to act fast. He jabbed the shark's eyes and it released him. Fox blindly reached out to push the shark away, but his right arm went straight into the great white's mouth. Razor-sharp teeth tore his skin. He immediately pulled his shredded arm out and wrapped his legs around the shark's body. He was safe from the shark's jaws, but he would die if he didn't get air. Fox let go of the shark and kicked to the surface. He gasped for breath. When he looked down, he saw the great white surging toward him through a cloud of blood.

Fox kicked the shark as hard as he could. To his relief, the shark turned its attention to the float and bit into it. Still attached to the float, Fox was dragged underwater. He felt the pressure of the water against his open wounds as the great white pulled him toward the ocean floor. Just as Fox was about to give up and let his lungs fill with water, the float line snapped. Fox used the last of his strength to reach the surface. As he struggled to breathe, he saw a boat speeding toward him. His rescuers got him to the hospital just in time. Rodney Fox had survived one of the worst shark attacks in history.

After the Attack

Fox's injuries were so severe that few people believed he would survive. After hours of surgery and over 360 stitches, Fox was on the road to recovery. Since the attack, Fox has devoted his life to studying great whites and other sharks.

Built to Kill

Great whites have patrolled Earth's oceans for nearly 20 million years. Today, the great white is one of the deadliest sharks on Earth. Its powerful jaws make it extremely dangerous. Most great whites have between five and seven rows of sharp, **serrated** teeth. When a tooth gets old or worn, it falls out. The one behind it moves forward to take its place. A great white can have more than 3,000 teeth. Their jagged edges rip flesh apart with ease. The great white's strong jaws crush bones with incredible force. A large great white can bite with a force of up to 4,000 pounds (1,800 kilograms). That's about 20 times stronger than a human can bite. The great white has one of the most powerful bites of any animal in the world.

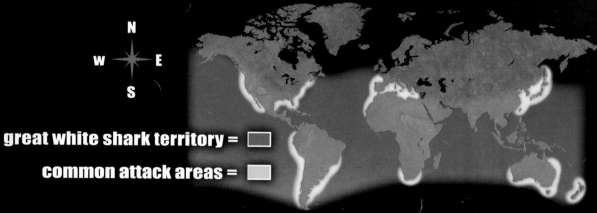

N
W — E
S

great white shark territory = ☐
common attack areas = ☐

sea lion

Great white sharks usually hunt seals and sea lions. They sneak up from below and sink their teeth into their prey. They shake their heads from side to side to tear off a mouthful of flesh. This first bite is usually **fatal**. Great whites stay close and wait for their prey to bleed to death before devouring their kill.

Hidden Hunter

The great white has a gray back and a white belly. These colors help it blend in with its surroundings so it can surprise prey. Animals looking up at a great white hardly notice its white belly against the sunlit water. Animals looking down at a great white can't see its gray back against the dark waters below.

Once in the water, there is no place to hide from a great white. The shark's sense of smell is so sharp that it can smell blood in the water from miles away. Great whites can smell a single drop of blood in 25 gallons (100 liters) of water. Their vision and hearing are just as sharp. They watch and listen for weak or injured animals.

Great whites also have special sensors that make them fierce predators. They can detect the faint **electric fields** of their prey through tiny bumps on their noses called **ampullae of Lorenzini**. The **lateral line** is another motion sensor. This is a system of tubes that runs under the great white's skin. Water flows through the tubes as the shark swims. If an object or animal gets close, the water vibrates and the shark knows prey is nearby.

The great white shark is the largest predatory fish in the world. Its size, strength, and speed make a fearsome combination. A great white can grow to be over 20 feet (6 meters) long and weigh as much as 5,000 pounds (2,270 kilograms). Its powerful muscles allow it to move quickly despite its size. A great white can cut through water at speeds of more than 15 miles (24 kilometers) per hour. Its tail moves slowly back and forth as it circles beneath unsuspecting prey. Then it raises its bullet-shaped head and charges toward the surface. The great white hits its target with so much force that both predator and prey shoot out of the water. As they fly through the air, the great white's deadly jaws slam shut on the prey. The shark falls back beneath the waves with its meal.

Megalodon

The megalodon terrorized the seas more than 15 million years ago. It was the biggest shark that ever lived. It grew to be 45 feet (14 meters) long and weighed 7,300 pounds (3,300 kilograms). Its teeth were 7 inches (18 centimeters) long. The megalodon could bite with a force of 20 times that of a great white.

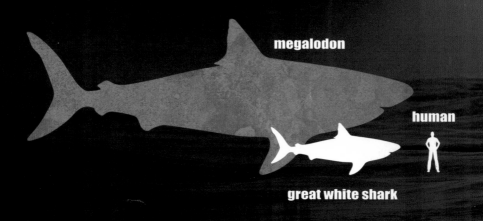

megalodon

human

great white shark

Great White Shark
Attacks

Scientists have developed several **theories** about why great whites attack humans. One theory is that they are curious. They take a test bite to investigate. When they find out that humans are bony and tough, most quickly let go and swim away. However, the test bite can severely injure or kill a human

Another theory is that great white sharks mistake humans for their usual prey. A surfer paddling out to catch a wave can look like a seal or sea lion. In **murky** water, a great white on the hunt might go after the dark shape of a swimmer or diver. These theories suggest that great white sharks attack humans only by accident.

surfer

sea lion

A more frightening theory exists.
Some people think great whites are
too smart to mistake humans for seals.
They believe that great whites attack
humans because they want to eat
them. Most scientists disagree with this
theory. They point to the low number
of fatal shark attacks. If great whites
enjoyed eating humans, they wouldn't
let their victims escape alive.

You can lower your risk of being
attacked by a great white if you follow
a few simple rules. Most importantly,
never swim alone. Stay out of the
water at night. This is when great
whites like to hunt. Make sure you
do not have cuts or wounds that are

see something you think might be a shark, leave the
...ght away. Stay calm and quiet because loud noises
...ashing attract great whites. If a shark attacks you,
...ck. Try to hit it in the eyes, **gills**, or nose. Use anything
...e with you as a weapon. If you are bitten, get
...l help immediately.

Attack Facts

- About 250 attacks by great whites have been confirmed worldwide since 1876. Of these, 65 resulted in the victim's death.

- Great whites have attacked about 126 people since the 1990s. About one out of every five attacks was fatal.

- In the United States, there have been 102 confirmed attacks by great whites. Twelve of these attacks were fatal.

- The great white sharks that patrol the waters around Australia are particularly deadly. They have attacked about 52 people. Over half of the victims were killed.

Great white sharks are powerful and dangerous animals. It is natural to be afraid of them, but they also deserve our respect. Great whites are not our enemies. They rarely kill humans. It is our job to protect great whites so we can learn more about them. If we stay out of their way, we can enjoy and explore the ocean waters without fear of an attack.

Glossary

ampullae of Lorenzini—tiny bumps on the noses of sharks that help them detect electric fields

electric fields—fields of energy created by movement; every living being has an electric field.

fatal—deadly

float—a device that floats in the water and is tied to a spearfisher; spearfishers use floats to hold the fish they've caught.

gills—organs on each side of a shark through which the shark breathes

lateral line—a system of tubes beneath a shark's skin that helps it detect changes in water pressure

murky—cloudy or dirty

serrated—having jagged edges

theories—ideas that try to explain why something exists or happens

torso—the section of the human body between the waist and neck

To Learn More

At the Library

Arnold, Caroline. *Giant Shark: Megalodon, Prehistoric Super Predator*. New York, N.Y.: Clarion Books, 2000.

Fox, Rodney. *Sharkman*. Norwood, Australia: Scholastic Australia, 2001.

Rake, Jody Sullivan. *Great White Shark*. Mankato, Minn.: Capstone Press, 2011.

On the Web

Learning more about great white sharks is as easy as 1, 2, 3.

1. Go to www.factsurfer.com.

2. Enter "great white sharks" into the search box.

3. Click the "Surf" button and you will see a list of related Web sites.

With factsurfer.com, finding more information is just a click away.

Index

The images in this book are reproduced through the courtesy of: Jim Watt/Photolibrary, front cover, pp. 10-11; Doug Perrine/Photolibrary, pp. 4-5; Carl Roessler/Photolibrary, pp. 6-7; Jeffrey L. Rotman/Photolibrary, p. 8 (left); ImageSource/Photolibrary, pp. 8-9; BW Folsom, p. 10 (top); Jon Eppard, p. 10 (bottom); Natalie Jean, pp. 11 (top), 17 (right); Mike Parry/ Getty Images, pp. 12 (top), 18-19; Masa Ushioda/Photolibrary, pp. 12-13; Klein-Hubert/ KimballStock, pp. 14-15, 16; Juan Martinez, p. 14 (bottom); Clay M. Rogers/Alamy, p. 17 (left); Jim Agronick, pp. 20-21.